ANIMAL TRACKERS
AROUND THE WORLD

IN THE JUNGLE

Tessa Paul

CRABTREE
Publishing Company

CRABTREE
Publishing Company

350 Fifth Avenue	360 York Road, R.R.4	73 Lime Walk
Suite 3308	Niagara-on-the-Lake	Headington, Oxford
New York, NY 10118	Ontario LOS IJO	England OX3 7AD

Editor **Greg Nickles**
Designer **Janelle Barker**
Consultant **Karen Jane Kemmis-Betty (M.Sc.)**

Illustrations
Andrew Beckett (cover background, track marks)
All other illustrations courtesy of Marshall Cavendish Partworks: Robin Budden/WLAA (pages 10, 27); Robin
Carter /WLAA (pages 18-19); John Cox/WLAA (pages 4-5, 22-23, 28-29); Barry Croucher/WLAA (pages 8-9, 25);
M. Donnelly/WLAA (page 7); Wayne Ford (pages 10-11); Matthew Hillier/WLAA (pages 8, 9); Steve Kingston
(pages 20-21); John Morris/WLAA (pages 6-7); Nick Pike/WLAA (pages 16-17); Peter David Scott/WLAA
(pages 12, 13, 26-27, 31); Valérie Stetton (pages 14-15); Kim Thompson (pages 24-25); Guy Troughton (page 25);
Simon Turvey/WLAA (page 17)

First printed 1998
Copyright © 1998 Crabtree Publishing Company

Cataloging-in-Publication Data

Paul, Tessa

In the jungle / Tessa Paul
p. cm — (Animal trackers)
Includes index.
ISBN 0-86505-591-2 (library bound)   ISBN 0-86505-599-8 (pbk.)
Summary: Introduces the physical characteristics, behavior, and tracks
of such jungle animals as the tiger, parrot, and chimpanzee.
1. Jungle animals—Juvenile literature. [1. Jungle animals. 2. Animal tracks.]
I. Title. II. Series: Paul, Tessa. Animal trackers.
QL112.P364 1998   j591.734   LC 98-10863
CIP

CONTENTS

IN THE JUNGLE

Jungles are colorful places that teem with life. Monkeys and orangutans swing through the trees. Birds fly, flashing their bright feathers among the leaves.

Jungles are also noisy places. Gibbons sing, chimpanzees yell, and parrots squawk. Each jungle has its own types of animals. This book tells you about some of the different animals that you can see in jungles around the world.

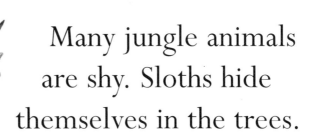

Many jungle animals
are shy. Sloths hide
themselves in the trees.
Tigers creep unseen through the
undergrowth. Pygmy chimpanzees make their
homes far from people and their villages.

The jungle provides animals with a plentiful
supply of food. Some eat fruit, and some
eat other animals. People know how to track
animals by looking for the plants they eat or
by finding the remains of their meal. In this
book, you will learn that jaguars go fishing.
You will discover that orangutans love to eat
honey, and capybaras like wet leaves.

TIGER

Tigers are meat eaters that live in the jungles of Asia. They are found in India, Malayasia, and parts of China. Tigers are the biggest cats in the world. They are different from most other cats because they do not often climb trees and they like water. Like most cats, however, tigers prefer to live alone. They sleep a great deal and hunt at night.

VISITING CALLS

Tigers live alone, but sometimes males and females meet to mate. A female tiger, the tigress, leaves a trail of scent marks through the jungle. When the male picks up her scent, he calls for her. She answers his roar. They spend four or five days together. Then the tigers leave one another. The tigress gives birth alone. She guards and feeds her young.

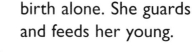

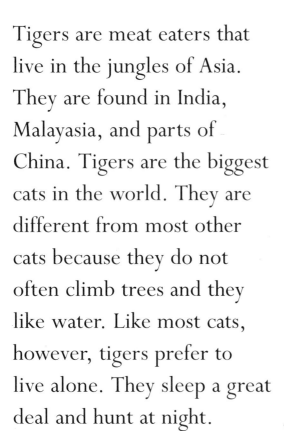

FOOTPRINT

Tigers have soft pads on their feet. They do not like walking on rough or hot surfaces.

MOVING DEN

A tigress may have one cub or as many as six. She keeps them hidden in the undergrowth and stays close to them. If she has to find food far from her cubs, she moves them. She carries them in her mouth to a new den nearer to the hunt.

A MOTHER'S CARE

Tiger cubs are born helpless and blind. The mother suckles them for almost five months, but looks after them and hunts their food for nearly two years.

Tigers are well suited to hunting in the jungle. They creep through the thick growth of plants looking for their prey. Their fur is difficult to see in the sun-striped shadows of the jungle. A tiger makes very little noise as it moves. When it is close to its prey, the tiger makes a powerful leap. It lands on the prey to bring it down. Its sharp teeth and claws tear at the prey's neck.

A BIG MENU

Tigers are strong and dangerous. Few animals are safe from their hunger. Monkeys, deer, rhinos, and wild pigs are all food for the tiger. It hunts even large animals such as young elephants and water buffalo. Tigers fear only humans and packs of dholes, the wild dogs of the Asian jungles.

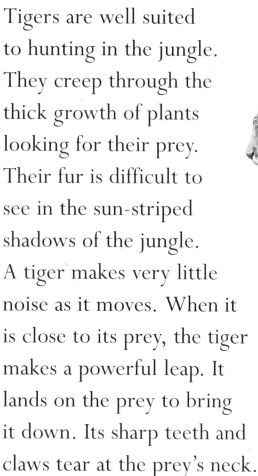

HIDDEN FOOD

Tigers drag their prey's body into long grass or the undergrowth. They hide it from scavengers such as jackals and vultures. A tiger has a rough tongue, and sharp teeth and claws. It uses these to take the skin off its prey before eating its flesh.

NIGHT LIFE

Tigers can see in the dark. Their eyes catch the palest beams of light. Their hearing is very good. Their rounded ears catch the slightest sounds. These special eyes and ears help tigers to hunt at night.

EARLY LESSONS

A tigress starts teaching her young to hunt when they are about six months old. She hides them where they can see her. By watching her, the cubs learn to hunt. After she makes a kill, she calls the cubs to join her. She lets them eat before she feeds herself.

MARMOSET

Marmosets eat fruit and insects, and live in the treetops of the Amazon jungle in South America. They are small and leap from tree to tree using their strong hind legs. Marmosets call to each other to keep in touch because they cannot always see each other through the leaves. Their musical cries sound like the songs of birds.

FINGERS AND CLAWS
A marmoset has claws on its fingers, but not on its thumbs. The claws help the marmoset grip branches.

FAMILY RULES
Marmosets live in groups led by one male and one female. The leaders are the only group members that breed. Their young, along with one or more male adults who are not related, make up the rest of the group. The leaders breed often, and a group may have up to fifteen members. Older family members help care for the very young. If others want to breed, they leave and start a new group.

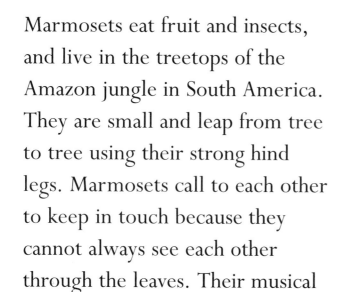

LITTLE FELLOW

Throughout South America, people keep marmosets as pets because the animals look cute and their fur is soft and silky. Their name comes from the French word "marmouset." This is a nickname meaning "little fellow."

A LENGTHY TAIL

The marmoset has a long tail. Marmosets use their tail to keep balance as they leap through the trees.

UNDER THE BARK

Marmosets are very light. They run across the thinnest branches, hunting the insects that eat tree leaves and blossoms. Marmosets also use the trees as a source of food. They scratch the bark with their teeth. When the sap oozes out, the marmosets lick it up.

SLOTH

Sloths live in the jungles of South America, where they hang upside down from branches. They have long, shaggy fur. Moths live in their fur, and algae grow on it. The algae give the fur a green tinge and make the sloth look like a bundle of old leaves. Sloths are slow. They creep along at only one mile per hour (under two kilometers per hour) and sleep sixteen hours a day. They creep down to the ground only once a week to urinate. Then they return to their branch.

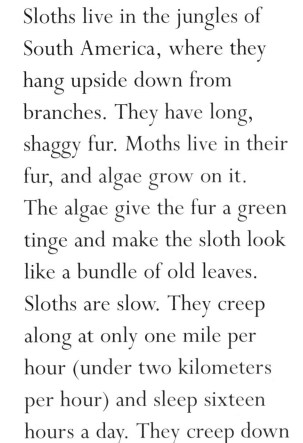

TIME TO GO

A female sloth gives birth to one baby. For the first month, it clings to its mother. It hides in her fur and lives on her milk. In the second month, the mother teaches it to eat leaves. After nine months, the mother forces the young sloth to leave.

TREES AND RIVERS

A sloth hangs by its legs. Its curved claws grip the branches. The front legs, which are longer than the hind legs, are used to reach for food. These front legs are also used to swim when the Amazon River floods. Sloths swim among the tree tops that poke above the water.

GREEN DIET

Sloths often like to eat the leaves of the trumpet tree. Sloths do not have real teeth. Their hard lips tug at leaves, and flat molars grind them until they are soft enough to swallow. Sloths may take an entire month to digest their food. Everything is slow in a sloth's life!

SUN LOVERS

Sloths like the warmth of the sun, so they climb to a branch where they can sunbathe.

CHASING FOOD

A sloth develops a taste for the leaves of one kind of tree, and will not eat from other kinds of trees.

13

MACAW

Parrots can be found in jungles all over the world. The macaw parrot lives in the Amazon jungle in South America. Macaws are swift fliers, but they do not fly great distances. They make short trips between their roosting and feeding areas. Like other parrots, macaws prefer to perch and shuffle on branches.

TO AND FRO
Parrots have two toes pointing forwards and two toes pointing backwards.

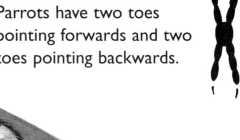

HELPLESS YOUNG
Macaws and other parrots nest in tree trunks and on branches. They pick hollows high above the ground. The mother sits on the eggs and the father brings her food. Their chicks are blind, featherless, and helpless at birth.

MIMICS
Parrots do not sing, but instead screech, whistle, and chatter. Parrots learn quickly to mimic human words. This trick, and their colorful feathers, make parrots popular as pets.

SLOW GROWING

The chicks of the macaw parrot spend over three months in the nest. During this time, both the mother and father feed the growing young.

TOOLS FOR EATING

Macaws and other parrots eat seeds, fruit, roots, nuts, and insects. The parrot's feet and curved beak are tools. With its feet, a parrot holds its food while it nibbles. It uses its beak to tear at fruit and roots, and to remove the shells from seeds.

LIVING TOGETHER

Macaw parrots live in groups called colonies. Together they talk and play. Pairs of males and females mate for life. Each mate helps preen and feed the other.

JAGUAR

Jaguars live in the remote parts of South American jungles. Not much is known about jaguars because they are few and hard to find. They live alone, not in groups that can be seen easily. Their patterned coat blends into the scenery. Jaguars come out only in the dim light of dawn and dusk to hunt.

TUCKED AWAY
Like most cats, the jaguar walks with retracted claws. This means the claws are pulled back into the paw.

CLAW MARKS

No one knows why a jaguar scratches at tree bark, leaving deep marks. The cat may be sharpening its claws, or the scratches on the tree may be a way of marking its territory. A jaguar scratches the same tree again and again.

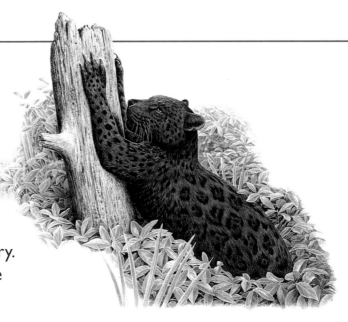

MATES AND CUBS

When they are ready to mate, male jaguars follow the scent marks left by a female and listen for her mating call. The males fight each other, and the strongest mates with the female. He takes no part, however, in rearing the cubs later. When she is about to give birth, the female seeks a hidden cave or hollow near water. Jaguars usually give birth to four cubs.

CHILD CARE

Jaguar cubs are blind at birth, and their coats do not have clear markings. They drink their mother's milk until they are about six months old. They stay with the mother and hunt in her range until they are nearly two years old.

The jaguar is a careful hunter. It is not as fast as other big cats, but it is patient. It sometimes follows its prey over long distances. It watches a herd for a long time before it pounces. A jaguar waits on river banks for other animals to come and drink. Then it jumps on them. Jaguars are also good at climbing trees. They hunt monkeys, birds, and sloths among the branches. Jaguars scavenge, too. This means they eat the meat of animals that they themselves have not killed.

DRY REFUGE

Jaguars rest comfortably on the branches of trees. During the rainy season when the Amazon River floods, they stay in the trees for long periods.

GONE FISHIN'

Jaguars are fishing cats. A jaguar stands on the river bank or even paddles in the shallows, gazing patiently into the water. If it sees a fish, the cat tries to swipe it out of the water or catch it in its paw.

JAW CRUNCHING

From a branch, this jaguar watches two peccaries, its prey. Jaguars have very strong jaws. They can crush a peccary's head or a tortoise's shell, or snap the neck of their prey. The rest of their body is also strong. Jaguars can drag bodies much heavier than themselves.

SECRET MEAL

The jaguar does not eat its prey at the site of the kill. It drags its meal into the undergrowth and eats, hidden from scavengers.

19

GIBBON

Gibbons can be heard yodelling and singing in the Asian jungles. Every day, each gibbon family sings together. The father starts, then the mother and young join in the chorus. They do this after they have swung through the trees in search of food. Males also sing to warn other gibbons away. This singing is more like shouting. It is called a "conflict-hoo."

SWINGING HOOKS

Gibbons have very long arms. Their hands do not hold branches, but instead hook over them. Gibbons swing through the jungle trees, racing along at 20 miles per hour (32 kilometers per hour). They have no tail.

STAND STRAIGHT

A gibbon's fingers are thin and strong. Gibbons stand and walk upright on their hind legs.

BLOWING VOICES

Gibbons have an air sac beneath their chin. When they sing, the sac blows up like a balloon.

FAMILY GROUPING

Male and female gibbons pair for life and live with up to four of their young. This family lasts for about five years. If a new baby causes the family to grow to more than six members, the older male children leave to find mates.

FOOD AND FUR

Gibbons eat figs, mangos, leaves, buds, flowers, and insects. Between meals, they groom each other.

21

BAT

Bats are found in jungles everywhere. They are the only mammals that can fly, and they can search for food over greater distances than other small mammals. Bats easily turn and dive in the air. A bat's heart, which is big for the size of its body, pumps large amounts of blood to help the bat's flying muscles.

THE ODD WALK

There are some types of bats that move on the ground. Sometimes they walk on all fours, as other animals do.

GRAB A BAT

Bats face danger in the Amazon jungle where birds and snakes hunt them. A bat hanging upside down in a tree is easy prey. A bat in flight is difficult to catch. An emerald tree boa, however, may still try to snatch a bat as it flies by.

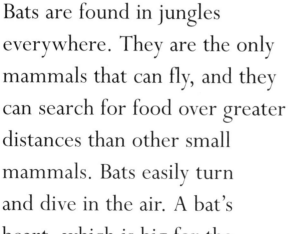

WRONG WAY UP?

Female and male bats live apart. They roost in caves or in shady trees in the jungle. Each sex forms a cluster, or group. There can be a dozen or a hundred bats roosting in one place. When not in flight, bats hang and sleep upside down. The females carry their youngest infant, which drinks its mother's milk even as she flies. Older infants are left in the roost.

CHO TRAVELERS

ome jungle bats eat fruit nd flowers. Others eat nsects, frogs, and lizards. hey search at night, most nding their way in the dark y "echolocation." As they y, they make small sounds. he sounds bounce off the urfaces of objects such as rees and rocks. The bat's ars measure the distance he sound travels. Then the at swerves to avoid the bject. Many bats can even ocate the fluttering insects.

MANY KINDS

Scientists are not sure how many kinds of bats exist. There are hundreds of wing shapes and faces. The top face shows a moustached bat. Its muzzle has whiskers. The lower face is that of a bulldog bat.

ORANGUTAN

The orangutan inhabits the jungles of Sumatra and Borneo, in Asia. It lives by itself and spends most of its time up in trees. The male has a loud roar called the "long call." He uses it to call for a mate or to warn other males to stay away. Orangutans also grunt, hoot, and sigh.

TENDER YEARS

A baby orangutan cling to its mother after it is born. It stays with h until it is six or even ten years old. A moth may have a second inf; when her first is three. Fathers play no part in family lif

OLD TRACKS

Only male orangutans spend time on the jungle floor. They grow so heavy they break branches when they swing on trees.

A FINE BED

Orangutans build nests high in the trees. They build a new one every night. They bend branches and bind twigs to make a bed with a roof, and then line it with leaves. They sleep on their sides or their back as humans do.

HUNGRY HABITS

Orangutans eat many types of fruit, and they love honey. They have very big appetites. An orangutan will sit all day in a durian tree. In that one day, it will eat all the fruit on the tree.

FACE TO FACE

A male orangutan is bigger than a female. He grows a beard and a moustache. The female's face is hairless. All orangutans have very long arms. The arms touch the ground when the animal walks.

CAPYBARA

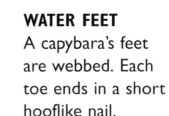

WATER FEET
A capybara's feet are webbed. Each toe ends in a short hooflike nail.

Capybaras live near rivers and lakes in tropical South America. They spend time in and out of the water. Capybaras sit belly-deep in water and eat, putting food into their mouths with their forepaws. They swim with their eyes, ears, and nostrils peeping above the water. If they are threatened, they form a circle in the water. Their young hide in the center.

WATER GARDENS

Capybaras spend much of the day on river bank. They graze on the lush grasses and plants that grow near the water, and pull water plants from the river bed to eat. Their leafy nests are built in the water.

SHARING MOTHERS

A female hides in a thicket to give birth. A litter of four cubs is usual. They are born with their eyes open. Capybara mothers feed each other's cubs.

SAFE NUMBERS

Capybaras live in herds. They protect each other from the jaguars and wild dogs that hunt them.

PYGMY CHIMPANZEE

Pygmy chimpanzees live in the Congo jungle in Africa. This jungle is so huge and dense that they are rarely seen. These apes live in family groups. They stay in the same group all their life. Every morning, the pygmy chimpanzees scramble from their nests in the trees. Calling and hooting, they race to the ground. They spend their day eating, resting, and playing.

WITH THUMBS
Chimpanzees have a humanlike thumb. This allows them to pick up and carry things.

BONDING
A group of pygmy chimpanzees has an equal number of adult males and females One male leads the whole group. Male and female adults care for the young within the group.

ROLE MODELS
Each male has his place in the group. Each obeys those who are stronger and more important. Males protect the females and young, and patrol the territory.

UTENSILS
Chimpanzees eat fruit, leaves, and insects. They use simple tools to find food. For example, they push grass stalks into an ants' nest to force the ants out. Stones are used to crack open nuts.

CLOSE TIES
The females have one infant at each birth. It stays by her side until it is about seven years old.

FOOD SEARCHES
Young males go foraging for food togther. The females prefer to forage alone, or with their young.

ROUGH HANDS

Chimpanzees spend a lot of their time in trees. They can, however, move easily on the ground. They stand upright. Their arms are long. The knuckles on their hands are hard. Chimpanzees lean on them to keep balance or when walking on all fours.

Chimpanzees are intelligent and skillful animals. Like humans, they care for their young for many years. They show affection by holding hands, embracing, and grooming each other. They know how to make simple tools. Pygmy chimpanzees even make fly whisks from bundles of leaves and twigs.

FIERCE ACTS

Males are aggressive. They chase away strange chimpanzees from other families. A male makes a show of his anger. His hair stands on end, he beats his chest, and he roars. He waves a stick in the air.

CHATTING AND SLEEPING

Pygmy chimpanzees work and play together. They have a language of hoots, murmurs, and grunts. If one screams in pain, the others rush to help it. At night, however, each builds its own nest and sleeps alone. Mothers take small infants into their nest with them. In the rainy season an entire group shelters in specially built day nests.

INDEX

GLOSSARY

Carnivore - An animal that eats mainly meat

Camouflage - Many animals have a coat or skin that blends with the color of the place where they live. This is called camouflage. Camouflage hides an animal from predators, or from prey it is trying to catch.

Colony - A large group of animals of the same kind living together is called a colony. These animals build their homes in one shared place.

Herbivore - An animal that feeds mainly on plants

Migrate - Animals migrate when they travel long distances to find food, warmth, or to breed.

Nocturnal - An animal that goes foraging or hunting at night

Plumage - The feathers covering a bird

Predator - An animal that hunts other animals

Prey – An animal that is hunted by another animal

Scavenger - An animal that eats what other animals have killed

Solitary – An animal that lives and hunts alone

1 2 3 4 5 6 7 8 9 0 Printed in the U.S.A. 7 6 5 4 3 2 1 0 9